DISCOVER 🐾 DOGS WITH
THE AMERICAN CANINE ASSOCIATION

I LIKE
YORKSHIRE TERRIERS!

Linda Bozzo

Published in 2017 by Enslow Publishing, LLC.
101 W. 23rd Street, Suite 240, New York, NY 10011

Library of Congress Cataloging-in-Publication Data
Names: Bozzo, Linda, author.
Title: I like Yorkshire terriers! / Linda Bozzo.
Description: New York, NY : Enslow Publishing, 2017. | Series: Discover dogs with the American Canine Association | Includes bibliographical references and index. | Audience: Ages 5 and up. | Audience: Grades K to 3.
Identifiers: LCCN 2016020791 | ISBN 9780766081673 (library bound) | ISBN 9780766081659 (pbk.) | ISBN 9780766081666 (6-pack)
Subjects: LCSH: Yorkshire terrier—Juvenile literature.
Classification: LCC SF429.Y6 B69 2017 | DDC 636.76—dc23
LC record available at https://lccn.loc.gov/2016020791

Printed in China

To Our Readers: We have done our best to make sure all websites in this book were active and appropriate when we went to press. However, the author and the publisher have no control over and assume no liability for the material available on those websites or on any websites they may link to. Any comments or suggestions can be sent by e-mail to customerservice@enslow.com.

Photo Credits: Cover, p. 1 Konstantin Gushcha/Shutterstock.com; p. 3 (left) Yevgen Romanenko/Shutterstock.com; p. 3 (right) Wavebreakmedia Ltd/Thinkstock; p. 5 tsik/Shutterstock.com; p. 6 Tatyana Domnicheva/Shutterstock.com; p. 9 yacobchuk/iStock/Thinkstock; pp. 10, 18 Felix Mizioznikov/Shutterstock.com; p. 13 (left) scorpp/iStock/Thinkstock; p 13 (right) © iStockphoto.com/jclegg (collar), Luisa Leal Photography/Shutterstock.com (bed), gvictoria/Shutterstock.com (brush), In-Finity/Shutterstock.com (dishes), © iStockphoto.com/Lisa Thornberg (leash, toys); p. 14 ka2shka/Shutterstock.com; p. 15 Tannis Toohey/Toronto Star/Getty Images; p. 17 Phase4Studios/Shutterstock.com; p. 21 Paravyan Eduard/Shutterstock.com; p. 22 © iStockphoto.com/Lunamarina.

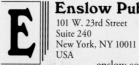

Enslow Publishing
101 W. 23rd Street
Suite 240
New York, NY 10011
USA
enslow.com

CONTENTS

IS A YORKSHIRE TERRIER RIGHT FOR YOU?

Yorkshire terriers, often called Yorkies, need very little space. They can live in almost any type of home.

Yorkshire terriers are small in size.

A DOG OR A PUPPY?

Yorkies are quick learners. They can be stubborn, so you will need patience when training. If training a puppy is not for you, an older Yorkie may be better for your family.

Due to their very small size, Yorkshire terriers are not the best choice for owners with very young children.

LOVING YOUR YORKSHIRE TERRIER

Your Yorkie will love for you to spoil him. Play with him. Lend him your lap. This small dog has a big personality!

EXERCISE

Yorkies like short walks on a **leash**. They do not need a lot of exercise. They are always ready to play games like **fetch**. Your Yorkie will like to be at your side at all times.

FEEDING YOUR YORKSHIRE TERRIER

Due to their small size, Yorkies should have food and water available at all times.

Dogs can be fed wet or dry dog food. Ask a **veterinarian (vet)**, a doctor for animals, which food is best for your dog and how much to feed her.

Give your Yorkie fresh, clean water every day.

Remember to keep your dog's food and water dishes clean. Dirty dishes can make a dog sick.

Do not feed your dog people food.
It can make her sick.

Your new dog will need:

a collar with a tag

a bed

a brush

food and water dishes

a leash

toys

GROOMING

Yorkies have silky hair that does not **shed**. This means their hair does not fall out. Because of her long hair, your Yorkie will need combing or brushing every day. Regular hair trims by a **groomer** are needed.

Use a gentle soap made just for dogs.

Your dog will need a bath every so often. A Yorkie's nails need to be clipped. A vet or groomer can show you how. Your dog's ears should be cleaned, and her teeth should be brushed by an adult.

WHAT YOU SHOULD KNOW ABOUT YORKSHIRE TERRIERS

Yorkies are bundles of energy. Yorkies are not recommended for families that have small pets like mice, hamsters, or rats.

Yorkies were bred to hunt rats and other small rodents. These small dogs have a big bark. This makes Yorkies good watchdogs.

You will need to take your new dog to the vet for a checkup. He will need shots, called vaccinations, and yearly checkups to keep him healthy. If you think your dog may be sick or hurt, call your vet.

A GOOD FRIEND

Yorkies can live anywhere from twelve to seventeen years. This means you can have many years of great fun with this four-legged friend.

NOTE TO PARENTS

It is important to consider having your dog spayed or neutered when the dog is young. Spaying and neutering are operations that prevent unwanted puppies and can help improve the overall health of your dog.

It is also a good idea to microchip your dog, in case he or she gets lost. A vet will implant a microchip under the skin containing an identification number that can be scanned at a vet's office or animal shelter. The microchip registry is contacted and the company uses the ID number to look up your information from a database.

Some towns require licenses for dogs, so be sure to check with your town clerk.

For more information, speak with a vet.

There are many dogs, young and old, waiting to be adopted from animal shelters and rescue groups.

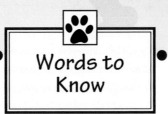
fetch To go after a toy and bring it back.

groomer A person who bathes and brushes dogs.

leash A chain or strap that attaches to a dog's collar.

rodents Small mammals with sharp front teeth.

shed When dog hair falls out so new hair can grow.

vaccinations Shots that dogs need to stay healthy.

veterinarian (vet) A doctor for animals.

Books

Finne, Stephanie. *Yorkshire Terriers.* Minneapolis, MN: Abdo Publishing, 2015.

Johnson, Jinny. *Yorkshire Terriers.* Mankato, MN: Smart Apple Media, 2013.

Websites

American Canine Association Inc., Kids Corner
acakids.com
Visit the official website of the American Canine Association.

National Geographic for Kids, Pet Central
kids.nationalgeographic.com/explore/pet-central/
Learn more about dogs and other pets at the official site of the National Geographic Society for Kids.

INDEX